EDGE
BOOKS

DIRT BIKES

Supercross Racing

by Tim O'Shei

Consultant:

Alex Edge
Associate Editor
MotorcycleDaily.com

Capstone
press

Mankato, Minnesota

Edge Books are published by Capstone Press,
151 Good Counsel Drive, P.O. Box 669, Mankato, Minnesota 56002.
www.capstonepress.com

Library of Congress Cataloging-in-Publication Data
O'Shei, Tim.
　　Supercross racing / by Tim O'Shei.
　　p. cm.—(Edge books. dirt bikes)
　　Summary: "Describes the sport of supercross racing, the types of motorcycles used,
major competitions, and athletes involved"—Provided by publisher.
　　Includes bibliographical references and index.
　　ISBN 0-7368-4366-3 (hardcover)
　　1. Supercross—Juvenile literature.　I. Title.　II. Series.
GV1060.1455.O75 2006
796.7'56—dc22　　　　　　　　　　　　　　　　　　　　　　2005005815

Editorial Credits

Connie Colwell Miller, editor; Jason Knudson, set designer; Kate Opseth,
　　book designer; Wanda Winch, photo researcher; Scott Thoms, photo editor

Photo Credits

Frank Hoppen, 14, 15, 24
Getty Images Inc./AFP/Cesar Rangel, 7; Lluis Gene, 21
Photo courtesy Motorcycle Hall of Fame Museum, 8
Steve Bruhn, cover, 5, 6, 11, 13, 17, 18, 22, 23, 25, 27, 28

1 2 3 4 5 6 10 09 08 07 06 05

Table of Contents

CHAPTER 1

Supercross Racing

The gate drops, and the race begins. Riders speed out on their motorcycles, spraying up dirt behind them. The riders struggle to gain speed as they race toward the first turn. Riders bump wheels and elbows. A few riders wipe out as they race through the turn.

These riders are competing in the sport of supercross. The riders race motorcycles on a dirt track. They face many challenges as they race to the finish line.

Learn about:
- Supercross tracks
- Bumps
- History

Supercross riders race against each other on a dirt track.

Supercross tracks feature bumps called whoops.

Obstacles and Stunts

Supercross riders zoom over a series of bumps and other obstacles on the track. They ride over bumps called whoops. These 2-foot (.6-meter) bumps are placed 6 to 9 feet (1.8 to 2.7 meters) apart. The track also has table top jumps. Table tops are flat on top. They stand 4 feet (1.2 meters) tall and 20 feet (6 meters) long. Riders can soar as high as a two-story house over the track's jumps.

On the final jumps of the 20-lap race, many riders entertain the crowd with daring mid-air stunts. Some riders kick their legs in the air. Others do handstands. Some riders even let go of the bike altogether. These tricks became so popular with fans that the sport of motocross freestyle was formed.

Riders' tricks at the end of supercross races turned into the sport of motocross freestyle.

Supercross rider Bob Hannah was popular in the 1970s and 1980s.

History of Supercross

In the early 1970s, Mike Goodwin had an idea for a new sport. He wanted to race motorcycles inside football and baseball stadiums.

Goodwin drew a picture on the back of a napkin. It showed a long, bumpy motorcycle track inside an oval-shaped stadium. Goodwin thought fans would enjoy watching racers speed around the curves and over bumps and jumps. Goodwin built the first track of this type in California.

"Super" Sport

In 1972, the first supercross race was held inside the Los Angeles Coliseum. Race organizers were nervous. They didn't know if the event would draw many fans. About 23,000 people attended "The Super Bowl of Motocross." Later, people began calling the events supercross races.

The popularity of supercross grew throughout the 1970s. By the early 1980s, supercross was the most popular motorcycle racing sport in the United States. Fans watched the sport on TV and read about it in magazines. Champions like Bob "Hurricane" Hannah became stars.

CHAPTER 2

Rules of the Sport

Most supercross competitions are held in North America. Riders come to North America from all over the world to become supercross stars.

The AMA Series

In 1974, the American Motorcyclist Association (AMA) created the AMA Supercross Series. This series of 16 races takes place each year from January to May. Each race in the series is held in a different city.

Learn about:
- The AMA Supercross Series
- Preparing for a race
- Scoring

The AMA Supercross Series has become popular worldwide.

The fastest riders in each race earn points. At the end of the season, the rider with the most points is the series champion.

Racers usually travel by airplane to the race locations. A truck driver hauls their equipment to the stadium or dome where the races will take place.

Before the Race

Each supercross track has different features. Riders face new challenges on every track.

To prepare for a race, riders study the track. They walk around and locate challenging curves and obstacles. They choose spots on the track that are safe for traveling quickly or for passing other racers.

Next, riders take a few practice laps. They want to make sure their bikes are working properly.

Time to Race

Supercross racers are divided into two racing groups based on the size of their engines. Motorcycle engines are measured in cubic centimeters (cc). The 250cc class is the most competitive. The 125cc class has less experienced riders. Many riders begin racing in the 125cc class. The best riders move up to the 250cc class.

Nearly 700 tons (635 metric tons) of dirt are needed to build a supercross track.

Riders have to battle each other to make it to the main event.

Riders must perform well to earn a place in the main event. First, riders compete in short races called heats. Each class has two heats. In each heat, 20 riders race for eight laps. The top four finishers from each heat move on to the main event. The rest of the riders go to the semifinals. These riders get another chance to qualify for the main event.

In the two semifinals, 16 riders race for six laps. The top five riders from each semifinal earn a spot in the main event.

The other 22 riders get one more chance to qualify for the main event. They ride in a race called the Last Chance Qualifier. The top two riders from this race ride in the main event.

The 20 riders in the main event race 20 laps. Every rider earns points. The first-place rider receives 25 points. The last-place rider receives one point.

The main event is a tough fight.

CHAPTER 3

Equipment and Safety

Supercross motorcycles look like other motorcycles. But they have special features that make them suitable for supercross racing.

Supercross Motorcycles

Racing teams are always looking for new ways to improve their motorcycles. The AMA has strict rules. Some bike parts cannot be changed.

Supercross bikes are lightweight. They weigh about 200 pounds (91 kilograms). Other types of dirt bikes can weigh as much as 300 pounds (136 kilograms).

Learn about:
- Supercross bikes
- Knobby tires
- Racing safety

Supercross motorcycles are built for racing on dirt tracks.

Lightweight bikes allow riders to sail through the air.

Standard dirt bikes are made of heavy steel parts. Supercross bike parts are made of lighter metals. Riders can travel more easily over obstacles on lightweight bikes.

Supercross bikes have a strong suspension system. A system of springs and shock absorbers helps cushion a bike over bumps and during rough landings.

Riders choose tires to fit their sport's needs. Supercross racers use knobby tires to grip the dirt. Some tires are made with the knobs close together. Riders use these tires on hard dirt tracks.

Safety

Supercross can be a dangerous sport. Riders wear safety gear, including a helmet, goggles, a full body suit, gloves, and boots. This gear helps protect riders from injuries during crashes. Still, most riders suffer injuries sometime in their careers.

CHAPTER 4

Supercross Stars

Some people believe supercross riders are among the best athletes in the world. Many riders lift weights, run, ride bicycles, and follow special diets. They also spend many hours on practice tracks.

Supercross is a young person's sport. Most pro riders are between 16 and 30 years old. Many riders began riding motorcycles at about 10 years old.

Learn about:

- Rider fitness
- Jeremy McGrath
- Current stars

Some supercross stars also helped make freestyle popular.

Many people consider Jeremy McGrath the best supercross racer ever.

The Sport's Best

Supercross champion Jeremy McGrath began riding motorcycles at age 3. He started racing at age 14. McGrath won seven AMA Supercross Series championships during his career. He became known as the "King of Supercross." McGrath retired in 2002 at age 31.

Ricky Carmichael is one of today's best supercross racers. Carmichael is a champion in both supercross and motocross. He was the top rider in both sports in 2001, 2002, and 2003.

In 2003, Ricky Carmichael won his third AMA Supercross Series championship.

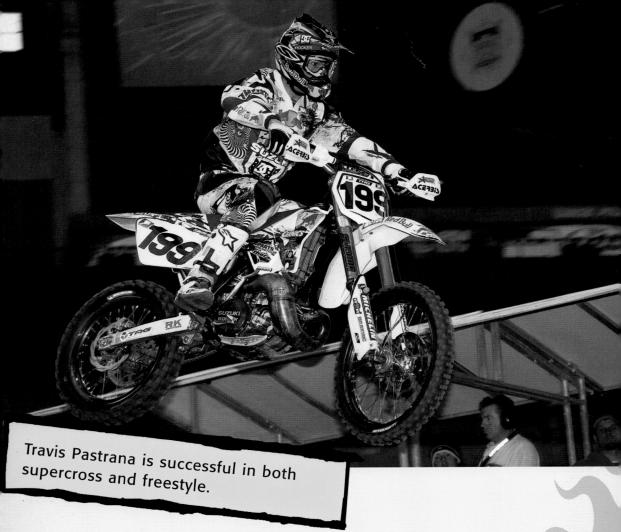

Travis Pastrana is successful in both supercross and freestyle.

Travis Pastrana is another popular supercross rider. Pastrana entertained fans by performing tricks while racing. He became one of the best in motocross freestyle. Pastrana has won many gold medals in freestyle at the X Games and Gravity Games.

Supercross racer Chad Reed grew up in Australia. In 2003, Reed was only seven points behind Carmichael in the standings. Reed won the 2004 AMA Supercross Series championship.

In 2004, Chad Reed finished in third place or better in every championship race.

Supercross rider James Stewart was born in 1985. Stewart was dominant in the 125cc class as a teenager. He moved up to the 250cc class in 2005. In April, he became the first African American to win a 250cc supercross main event. Many people expect Stewart to be a star for a long time.

Other riders will join Stewart to become the next group of supercross stars. Every new season, each racer has a chance to be the best.

James Stewart is known for his flashy supercross riding style.

Supercross racers make money by agreeing to use certain equipment.

Racing Business

Supercross racing is big business. The best riders can make hundreds of thousands of dollars. A few riders even make millions. Most of this money comes from companies paying the riders to use and advertise their products. Racers who have a deal with a manufacturer are called "factory riders." Those who don't are called "privateers."

Glossary

freestyle (FREE-stile)—a motocross event that includes jumps and tricks

heat (HEET)—a short race that decides which riders make it to the main event

obstacle (OB-stuh-kuhl)—something that gets in the way or prevents someone from doing something

qualify (KWAHL-uh-fye)—to try to earn a spot in the main event by finishing high in heats

stadium (STAY-dee-uhm)—a large building in which sports events are held

suspension (suh-SPEN-shuhn)—a system of springs and shock absorbers that cushions a hard landing

whoops (WOOPS)—a series of bumps on a supercross track

Read More

Freeman, Gary. *Motocross.* Radical Sports. Chicago: Heinemann, 2003.

Herran, Joe, and Ron Thomas. *Motocross.* Action Sports. Philadelphia: Chelsea House, 2004.

Parr, Danny. *Dirt Bikes.* Wild Rides! Mankato, Minn.: Capstone Press, 2002.

Sievert, Terri. *James Stewart: Motocross Great.* Dirt Bikes. Mankato, Minn.: Capstone Press, 2006.

Internet Sites

FactHound offers a safe, fun way to find Internet sites related to this book. All of the sites on FactHound have been researched by our staff.

Here's how:

1. Visit *www.facthound.com*
2. Type in this special code **0736843663** for age-appropriate sites. Or enter a search word related to this book for a more general search.
3. Click on the **Fetch It** button.

FactHound will fetch the best sites for you!

Index